INDIAN NATIONS

The Story of the Seminole

About the Book

The people we know as Seminoles have a history that is remarkably parallel to that of the rest of us Americans. Most of our ancestors came from many nations, fleeing conflict and persecution, and settled in a new world that promised freedom and opportunity. The ancestors of the Seminoles were Indians from various tribes who fled from conflict and the persecution of the white man to settle in Florida. The Seminoles as a tribe are as new as the United States as a nation, and they have fought for their freedom and new identity as fiercely as did the American colonists.

The Story of the
SEMINOLE

by the Editors of
COUNTRY BEAUTIFUL
Text by Marion E. Gridley

Illustrations by Robert Glaubke

G. P. Putnam's Sons   *New York*

in association with Country Beautiful Corporation,
Waukesha, Wisconsin

Contents

Introduction **8**

1. The Seminoles **11**

2. Life in a Seminole Village **17**

3. Life in a Seminole Chickee **21**

4. How the People Dressed **25**

5. Growing Up **29**

6. Folktales **33**

7. The Stickball Game **37**

8. The Medicine Man **41**

9. The Green Corn Dance **44**

10. Some Famous Seminoles **48**

11. The Fighting Ends **53**

12. The Seminoles Today **55**

Index **61**

The Story of the

SEMINOLE

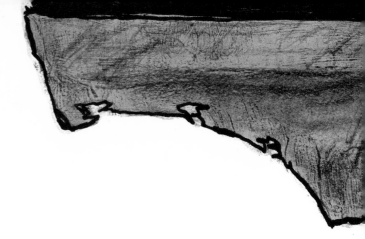

Introduction

Today we identify the Seminoles with Florida, although the tribe has not always lived there. Very little is known about the Indians who did live in Florida at the time of the coming of the Spaniard.

Spanish explorers entered the New World through the peninsula which they named Florida, or "land of flowers." The many Indians who were living there seemed much like the people of Mexico and Central America. It is possible that, very far back in years, they may have come from that region we now call Latin America. Tribes of the Southeast tell of a long journey from west to east and of crossing the Mississippi River.

The Spaniards killed most of the Florida Indians and sold others into slavery in Cuba and the West Indies. Only a few survived, to join later with the Seminoles.

The Seminoles are a mixture of stragglers from other Indian tribes that were persecuted by the white-skinned newcomers. Although new as a tribe, the Seminoles developed their own culture and have kept their own manner of life and customs into recent times. The Seminoles are one of the most distinctive of all Indian groups.

1
The Seminoles

The Seminole tribe did not exist as a tribe until around the time of the American Revolution. It was made up of small groups of Indians who began to move southward from Georgia and Alabama in the early 1700's. Some of these were refugees from tribal wars. Some had been caught in the conflict between the Spanish and English, who were fighting for power and control of the riches of the New World. Others had separated from the mighty Creek nation, perhaps because they preferred to hunt rather than to farm as the Creeks did, perhaps because they disagreed among themselves.

When these mixed people came to Florida, they found few Indians there. By then most had been destroyed. The newcomers absorbed the few that were left, and all banded together as a tribe. Seminole means "runaway," and this was the name by which these Indians came to be known, for this is what they were. They had run away from another life.

The Seminoles spread over northern Florida. They were an industrious people, and they occupied the richest land in the area. In time they became quite well-off. They hunted, fished, farmed, and raised some horses and cattle. They liked to trade and exchanged skins, furs, dried fish, beeswax, honey, and bear oil with the Spanish for coffee, sugar, and tobacco.

They were tireless travelers, constantly coming and going over well-worn trails which led to other villages where they visited friends and relatives.

The Seminoles were fearless warriors. They refused to surrender in battle but fought until they could fight no more or until they could escape into the woods and swamps they knew so well. Once away, they were out of sight.

In the early days of American settlement and colonization, Indian tribes generally sided with those on whom they depended for trade. In 1763, the Spanish lost Florida to England. At the end of the Revolutionary War, the land was returned to Spain. The Seminoles, therefore, had friendly relations with both countries.

The Americans, colonizing along the Florida-Georgia border, did not forget that the Seminoles had helped the English during the war. They were further angered because the Indians were taking in the black slaves who escaped from Southern plantations and protecting them. The Seminoles were a proud people. They would not be slaves, and therefore they would help others escape from slavery. The slaves lived among them something like tenant farmers.

There were increasing clashes between the Americans and the Seminoles, especially over the escaped blacks. Plantation owners attempted to invade the Indian villages to seize their "property," and the Indians strongly resisted. During the War of 1812, an army was sent into Seminole country by the Americans, who feared that the English would play upon their former friendship with the tribe and make use of this.

Seminole villages were burned and plundered. Herds of horses and cattle and thousands of deerskins were taken, and the people were scattered. In 1817, General Andrew Jackson was sent to Florida with troops to war upon the Seminoles. While in pursuit of the Indians, Jackson so weakened Spanish authority that Florida was finally ceded to the United States in 1819.

In 1823, a treaty was made by which the Seminoles agreed to give up 32,000,000 acres of land for a 4,000,000-acre reservation in central Florida. All the tribe were to live there, and were promised there would be no harassment if they abided by United States laws.

In addition, they were given farm implements, livestock to replace the destroyed animals, food rations, and funds for a school. A yearly payment of $5,000 to the tribe was to continue for twenty years.

The sudden and drastic change in their way of life brought great hardship to the Indians. The land was poor, waterlogged, and not at all suited for farming. There were few places to get good drinking water. Those who came late to the reservation could not plant crops, for it was past the season. There was not enough land

for the large number of people. So began a struggle for survival. In a short time, the Indians were raiding settlements for food, for they had none of their own.

As more and more Americans pushed into Florida, pressure increased for the removal of the Indians. It became a government policy that all Indians were to be sent west to Indian Territory, later to become the state of Oklahoma.

A few of the Seminoles agreed to go, and a new treaty,

14

which gave them a payment of $15,400 for the Florida lands, was signed. Most of the people were determined to stay in their homes, no matter what the cost. They flatly refused to leave, and war broke out anew.

The Indians fought bitterly and fiercely for nearly eight years. They never had more than 1,500 fighting men against several thousand soldiers, who drove them from place to place but who never quite caught up with them. At last they were subdued, however, as other

Indians had been before them, and the removal to the West began.

One small band of resisters still held out. They were not conquered, and they signed no treaty. They fled into the swamps, where they lived off the land, ready to run or fight to the death. Mothers hid their small children in pits and visited them only at night because they were so afraid that the soldiers would find them.

Since it was impossible to contact the Indians, they were left alone, so long as they stayed in the swamps, which we now call the Everglades.

In order to adjust to the new conditions, the manner of life of the Indians had to change, and new skills had to be developed. Before they came to the Everglades, the Seminoles had lived in log cabins like those of the first settlers. These were not suitable for the hot, humid swamps. The Indians designed open huts thatched with palm leaves, which were much more comfortable and which blended into the swamp growth.

There were no trails to travel, so the Seminoles became a boat people. They knew the waterways of the swamps as well as they had once known the land paths. Where others would easily become lost in the maze of water, palm trees, and long grass, sometimes taller than a man, the Indians found their way without difficulty.

Hating the white man for all the suffering that had come to them, the Indians stayed hidden and would accept no overtures of friendship. They did not encourage or welcome visitors, and they left their villages only when necessary. They made no attempt to adopt any of the white man's ways or to learn his language. They made do with very little, asking only to be left alone. They had found peace.

2
Life in a Seminole Village

Wild and desolate, the Everglades is also a place of
vivid color and beauty. Tall palms and cypress trees are
hung with long chains of Spanish moss. At their bases
grow giant ferns. There are beautiful flowers and colored
tropical birds and butterflies.

This is the haunt of the deer, the otter, the panther,
the bear, and smaller animals. It is the home of the wild
turkey, of the snow-white egret and the stately heron.
Fish swim in the dark-green waters. Alligators bask on
the sunny banks or slip into murky pools. Many kinds
of snakes wind their way through the tall, waving grass.

The Seminoles have been a part of the strange Everglades for more than 250 years. Their small villages of
only a few houses are built on clumps of higher ground
called hammocks, or hummocks, the only dry land in the
swamps.

When they first came to Florida, the Indians lived in

towns with houses grouped around an open square, which was the pattern of Southeast living. In the center of the square there was a building which was like a community center and which at one time had been a temple.

Each town had its own head chief, but there was no single leader for the tribe. To become a chief, a man had to prove that he was able and wise. He had to gain and hold the respect of his village.

The swamp houses were called chickees. So well were they concealed that it was possible to pass close by without seeing them. There was little sound to give the village away. The people spoke in soft, low voices as though they were whispering. The children were trained to play quietly without any yelling or screaming, and they were not allowed to cry.

A sudden movement or sound from a bird or animal warned the people that someone was coming. Then the village became very still while the Indians waited to see who it was—friend or foe.

Because a boat was necessary to life in the Everglades, the Seminoles taught themselves to make dugout canoes. For these, they used the large cypress trees which were blown down by the powerful hurricane winds. When the tree dried out, the men began the work of peeling off the bark and hollowing out the trunk.

The Indians had long been in close contact with Europeans, so they had some metal tools, among them knives and axlike blades called adzes. Burning embers were placed on the log, and the charring wood was scraped away with metal blades or with sharp shells.

The canoes were wider than the bark canoes of the Northern tribes, and they were shallow, for swamp water isn't very deep. The sides were rounded, and the front of the canoe came to a point and curved upward so that it rose out of the water. The bottom of the boat was nearly flat.

The Indians had no patterns to follow, and they could measure only by eye. Still, the finished boats floated with perfect balance and skimmed through the water with ease. They were large enough to carry a whole family. The man of the household stood up and poled the dugout through the water, moving it along as silently and as quickly as the swimming fish. It could be poled through the high, thick grass growing in solid walls. It was perfect for swamp travel and for hunting alligators or spearing fish. In their dugouts, the Seminoles even made their way to Cuba.

3
Life in a Seminole Chickee

The Seminole chickee was a platform built about three feet from the ground, open on every side, and with a palm leaf roof. There was no furniture. The families slept on mats on the floor; the baby slept in its own hammock. The sleeping mats were rolled up in the daytime, and the people sat on the floor, where they ate, sewed, played games, or carried on other activities.

Close to each house was a small garden. With so little usable land, not much food could be raised. The Indians grew some corn, pumpkins, tomatoes, sweet potatoes, cowpeas, and sugarcane. There was just enough raised for need. Bananas, guavas, and other fruits grew wild,

21

and the bud of the cabbage palm was eaten raw or cooked.

A favorite food was coontie, made from the roots of a swamp plant which were pounded into flour and then made into cakes.

The one staple food was sofkee. This is a mush made of corn pounded to coarse grains in a large, partly hollowed-out log. The corn grits were boiled to make a thin porridge. This was always part of a Seminole meal.

Food was cooked over an open fire. The fire was built in the center of the village and was used by all the

families living there. A shelter protected it from rain, and this shelter was also used as a kitchen house. Hanging from the roof were the pots used for cooking and meat which dried in the smoke of the fire. Another shelter was used for the preparation of food.

The Seminole fire was unusual. Eight or ten logs were placed like the spokes of a wheel with the fire in the center. As the inner ends of the log burned away, the logs were pushed up into the flame. The people sat on the unburned ends, for these made good benches. Food was kept warm by being placed between the logs near the fire.

The food was boiled in large iron kettles. Several kinds of food went into the kettle at one time for a savory stew. This is the Indian way of cooking, for there were not many kettles in which different foods could be cooked separately. Meat, fish, and turtles were broiled alongside the fire.

The cooked food was placed on large palm leaves or in shell dishes. It was set in one place, and the people gathered around while it was blessed. Then the people carried their share to their chickees, where it was eaten.

The Seminoles did not make pottery, but shells were used in many ways—as drinking cups, knives, and garden hoes.

When the people saw the sawgrass pollen hanging in the air, they began to pack up their belongings for a move inland to higher ground. The pollen was always visible for several days before a hurricane struck. The people stayed away from their homes until it was safe to return.

4
How the People Dressed

When the Seminoles first came to Florida, they wore buckskin clothing as other Indians did farther to the north. The Florida climate was too warm for such clothes, and so the people changed to loose-fitting long garments made of a lightweight cloth which they got from traders. Even though any clothing was warm, the body had to be covered because of the millions of insects and mosquitoes. These swarms of mites bit any exposed skin.

Clothes were later made of calico, gingham, and cotton. They were decorated with stripes of colored braid. Some had designs cut out of cloth and sewn around the borders of the long skirts worn by both men and women. The women's skirts swept the ground, and with them they wore capelike blouses. The men wore a one-piece long shirt which came down to the knees or a little below.

A man wore two bandannas around the neck and a tur-

ban with plume feathers on his head. A woman wore
many heavy strings of beads around her neck like a high
collar. No woman would appear without her beads. They
sometimes weighed as much as 25 pounds.

It is said that the Indians of Peru once wore clothing
like the Seminole Indians. It is also said that the women's
dresses were influenced by those of the Spaniards. The

clothing protected the people not only from insects, but from the sharp-edged grasses and spiny plants which abounded in the area.

The children dressed exactly as their parents did, and all went barefooted. The Seminoles did not ever wear moccasins.

Then something happened to change the whole style

of dress and to make it one of the most unusual of Indian costumes in America. Somehow, sometime, a trader introduced the Seminoles to the sewing machine. The women seized on this with great eagerness, and it was not long before every house had its hand-turned sewing machine.

With the introduction of the sewing machine, the dress style of the Seminoles completely changed. The stitched-on braids and designs disappeared. Brightly colored cotton cloths were cut into hundreds and hundreds of small pieces. These were sewn together again in horizontal bands of delicate and complicated designs. The strips, each with its own design pattern, were then sewn together with a band of solid color between them. From this remade cloth, shirts and skirts were fashioned. There might be as many as 5,000 small bits of cloth in one skirt. Seminole clothing was no longer patchwork-decorated. It was made entirely of patchwork, and each piece of clothing was a work of art.

Each dress or shirt was different, for the design stripes were never the same, and the range of designs was astonishing. In spite of the strong, bright colors and the unusual combinations, the clothing did not look garish but beautiful. The skill with which the tiny pieces were sewn together is unbelievable.

In the past, women wore their hair loose and flowing or piled in a knot on top of the head. Then a style developed in which the woman rolled her long hair over a piece of cardboard so that it was like a hat with a wide brim. It served the same purpose as a hat, for the eyes were shaded from the glare of the sun.

In their gay-colored clothes, the Seminoles were like the vivid birds and butterflies of their Florida home.

5
Growing Up

When a Seminole child was born, a small bag of fragrant herbs was tied around its neck. This was meant to ward off evil spirits and to keep the child in good health.

The baby was not put in a cradleboard like the children of other tribes. The baby was carried in the arms or on the hip. When the mother was at work, or at night, it was placed in a hammock and swung to sleep. When the mother was working, she swung the hammock by means of a thong attached to her foot.

As soon as the child could walk, it began to learn the ways and customs of the Seminole people. A little girl, by the time she was six, knew how to run the sewing machine. She made her own clothes and those of her dolls. She helped her mother sort scraps of cloth, string beads, and prepare meals.

When she was eight years old, she mothered the younger children and carried the baby on her hip, even when she played. The baby was always with her, and she shared her food with it.

When a girl was twelve years old, she was given a string of glass beads to wear around her neck. Strings were added with each birthday until the beads covered the neck to the chin. It was considered highly improper and immodest not to wear these beads, and no girl or woman would be seen in public without them.

After a girl became forty, the bead strings were removed one by one with each birthday. The last string was buried with the woman when she died.

At fourteen, the girl was ready for marriage, and by then she was an accomplished housewife. Her husband was chosen for her by her family.

Seminole boys learned to hunt, fish, pole the dugout canoes, and even make them, when they were quite small. When they were twelve, they, too, were accomplished in tribal activities. They were considered men, and they had all the rights and privileges of any man in the village.

All children were strictly brought up. A child who was naughty had his arm scratched with a needle or sharp thorn until the blood was drawn. Children were taught to tell the truth at all times and to answer questions with a straight "yes" or "no." When there were visitors in camp, they were made to be quiet, and crying was quickly hushed up. Otherwise, the children were merry and happy among themselves.

As they grew up, they learned that there were relatives who must be shown great respect. With these relatives there could be no joking, and they were seldom

spoken to. A boy's uncle on his mother's side was his trainer and counselor, and he was looked up to and obeyed in every way.

The children were also taught that they must never try to outdo or excel over another. In their games, there could be no rivalry, but players tried to help other players and did not try to overcome them.

The Seminoles had many folk songs which were taught to the children. These had been sung for generations. There was one about a horned owl, and one about a little red rabbit, and another about a little raccoon.

Then there were the stories that went with everything. The storyteller was an important person in the Seminole village. When stories were told, the whole family gathered around to listen. Sometimes a child would be asked to repeat a story that had been told to prove that he had paid attention and that he understood what the story taught.

6
Folktales

Night was the time for storytelling. The family would sit on the chickee floor, and the grandfather or some older man would start the stories. The people listened very quietly. Now and again they would hear the cry of a panther, the glumph-ing sound of an alligator, or the call of a night bird swooping through the dark.

Some of the stories were about the stars, which were always very bright and so large that it seemed as though one could reach out and touch them. The storyteller would point out the Milky Way, which the Seminoles and all of the animals would walk when they died. The Milky Way is the road to a new home in the West where Breath Maker lives.

The storyteller would point out the stars which we call

the Big Dipper. These were the outline of a Seminole
boat, he said. Once a Seminole on a journey lost his way
and found himself in the sky. Only his boat remains to
remind other Seminoles of him.

34

Once the Breath Maker set out on a journey with seven Indian men, the storyteller said. They walked a long, long way—all the way to the end of Florida. Breath Maker taught the men how to fish. He showed them the coontie plant and taught them how to use it for food.

Then he blew his breath into the sky and made the Milky Way. He left the Indians and went to his home. He told the people that when one of them died, if he were a good person, the Milky Way would shine brightly to light the way to the western land.

Another story was about the silver moss which hangs from the trees in Florida. This story was about a Seminole girl who was to marry a chief of the Creeks.

The Creeks and the Seminoles had been at war, and many young men of both tribes had been killed. The older people wanted the marriage to take place, for they felt it would put an end to bloodshed and bring peace and friendship once more.

On the morning of the marriage day the Creeks came down from the north. They were proud men, and lordly of bearing. The Seminoles were proud, too, and they did not like the manners of the Creeks. Soon there were angry words and then blows, and the fighting began again. Many more were killed, among them the chief who had come to claim his bride.

To show her grief and mourning, the girl cut off her long strands of hair and hung them in the branches of the trees. Then she took her own life.

As the years went by, the hair turned silver and spread from tree to tree. The story of the maiden has remained with the Seminoles.

7
The Stickball Game

In a field beside a waterway, the Seminoles and the Creeks have come together for a game of stickball. This is not just a game, but a contest to settle a quarrel. Whichever team wins the game will be the victor in the argument as well.

From miles around, the Indians have come to watch and to bet on their team. The long dugout canoes bring the families and even the family dog. Stickball has been a favorite sport for generations.

Sometimes the Indians called this game "the little brother of war." It took the place of going to war to settle tribal differences. But sometimes warfare broke out when the game was over, if the losing tribe refused to abide by the decision or to consider matters settled.

The two teams come onto the field and put up their goalposts while the people find good seats. They all are very excited, for this is a dangerous game. Anything goes in the course of play. There are twenty men on each team, but few are left when the game is over.

This game was popular among all Eastern tribes. In the North, the French gave it the name of lacrosse. In the South, it was played a little differently, but the game was still pretty much the same.

Stickball is often called the "granddaddy of all American ball games." Like basketball, it is played with a jump ball in the center of the field. After each score, the play takes up again with another jump ball in the center. The ball is quite small.

Like football, there is a form of tackling and blocking. The playing sticks are made of hickory wood. A netting made of laced deerskin thongs is at one end. The ball can be touched only with the playing rackets. The players may bat the ball or run with it in the stick nets. They may also throw the ball with their sticks. Only one ball is used, and to gain possession and control of it is what the game is all about.

Whoever has the ball must throw it through the goalposts of his team. The opposing team must try to take

the ball away or to block the throw. The field is long, but the players are able to throw the ball for a very great distance. They can catch the ball with their sticks with great skill as it comes whizzing through the air.

There are no time outs, and a player may not leave the game unless he is knocked out. The game continues until one side has scored 100 points.

When it is time to start, a hush falls over the crowd. The players group in the center of the field. They wear no clothing but breechcloths, although some wear tails made of white horsehair or quills.

The medicine man comes forward with the hard wood ball, about the size of a walnut. Now he tosses it into the air, and the fight begins as the players try desperately to move the ball toward their far-off goals.

At one side of the field, the scorekeepers sit with their sharpened sticks. A stick is pushed into the ground each time a point is scored until there are 50 for each team. Then they are removed one by one until the winning side has no sticks left.

At each set of goalposts, a bowl of "medicine" holds a piece of turtle hide. This is to attract the ball, and the playing sticks have been smeared with this same "medicine." The ball itself holds a worm which is believed to make it invisible to the other side.

As rough as the game is, the players try not to hurt one another, and there are no foul plays. The important thing is to win. Seminole boys learn to play this game as soon as they can run.

Stickball is still played, although the score is now for 20 points only, and not for 100 points. Although some of the old rituals remain, the game is purely for recreation. It is an exercise in good sportsmanship.

8
The Medicine Man

Among all people there are certain beliefs and customs which have to do with their lives in time of sickness.

The Seminole medicine man conducted the ceremonials which were used at times of birth or death, or when a child became an adult, or for mourning. Mainly he healed the sick, and because of this, he was a very important person in tribal life.

Not every man could become a medicine man. Only those whom the medicine man selected from among the boys and whom he said were worthy could be trained in this art. They had to be willing and able to go through long and hard study to achieve the several degrees.

The medicine man might not reach his first degree until he had studied for at least seven years, and with this degree he could do only certain things. He might not reach the highest and final degree, when all knowledge was his, until he had become quite an old man.

The medicine man was a spiritual healer. Other Indians could gather herbs and plants for simple treatments, but they were not medicine men.

41

The medicine man cured through chanting or singing certain magical verses. He performed certain rituals, and he could control all of nature, the winds and the storms, the ghosts that wandered around the world, and the ghost of his patient. He could drive away the disease spirits. He understood the meaning of dreams, and he treated a patient according to what he dreamed and how it was interpreted.

When the medicine man decided what was causing his patient's illness, he gathered the needed herbs and mixed them together. The herbs could be picked only from the north and east sides of the plant. He sang the proper songs and blew on the medicine through a cane tube as it brewed. He and his patient faced east while the ceremony was taking place.

The medicine man was the guardian of all war medicine. This was said to be so powerful that it was not kept in the camps or villages but was hidden away in a secret place. The war medicine was a powder of some kind, and it was kept in small deerskin bags. These were opened only at the Green Corn Dance, and great care was taken that none of the powder was spilled.

The war medicine could not be touched with the hand but was scraped into a pile with a quill feather from a buzzard's wing. Women could never touch or come near the war medicine, but women could treat other women and children in minor illnesses.

If a medicine man was unable to draw back the ghost of his patient and death took place, he had to go through purification ceremonies. He could not try to heal again for four weeks. If he did not cleanse and purify himself, he had to wait four months before he could make medicine again.

9
The Green Corn Dance

There were two very important ceremonials among the Seminoles. These came down from the traditions of other tribes, whose members made up the Seminoles.

One was the Autumn Hunting Dance. In the autumn, the first deer killed in that season was burned in the woods where it fell. This was thought to bring health to any member of the hunter's family who might be ill. It would also bring him forgiveness for any wrong things that he might have done.

During the ceremonial time, a small part of every deer killed near the village grounds was burned before the meat was cooked for eating. The meat was stewed, and the broth was sprinkled over the graves of women and children.

The most important ceremony of all was the Green Corn Dance. This was held when the corn was ripe. It was the Seminole New Year celebration.

For the New Year, every house was cleaned and new roofs were made. Clothes, tools, and weapons were burned and replaced with new ones.

The village fires were put out, and the fireplace was sprinkled with clean white sand. Then the lighting of the

New Fire took place. Of all ceremonies, this held the greatest religious significance.

In the center of the town, four large logs were placed to form a cross. The outer ends of the logs pointed to the four directions of the earth. When the dawn streaked the sky, the Fire Maker faced the rising sun. He struck a piece of flint and lighted a bundle of dried grass. As it burned and burst into flame, it was placed in the center of the logs, and the New Fire was lighted.

The Indians danced around the fire singing ceremonial songs. Attached to their legs were rattles made of coconut shells with pebbles inside. The soft sound they made kept time with the chanting.

When the dancing ended, each woman was given an ember from the New Fire, and with it she lit her house fire again.

So the New Year began. The festival lasted for five days, and it was a time for rejoicing and for thanksgiving. All tribal problems were considered and discussed and acted upon, and marriages took place.

During the rites, the people drank a mystic brew made from the leaves of a holly tree. The brew, called the black drink, was believed to cleanse internally and to purify the people from all bad acts and thoughts. It was also believed to give warriors great strength and bravery. When two people drank the drink together, a pledge of friendship was made which could never be broken.

On the second day of the festival, the feather dance was held. Just before this took place, there were the ceremonial scratching rites. Women were not allowed to take part in this. Snake fangs or sharp claws were used to scratch the bodies of those taking part until blood was drawn. This purified the body.

During the festival, also, a sacred ball game in which
both young men and women took part was played.

Ceremonial offerings were made to the Great Spirit
whom the Seminoles called Ishtohollo, or Mighty Good-
ness, or Breath Maker. They also called him Yo-He-Wah,

or Evil Spirit, for he was a two-sided god. He brought
all good things to man, but he also brought evil. His
name was never spoken. It was mentioned only in the
chants which were sung around the sacred fire when
ceremonies took place.

10
Some Famous Seminoles

"You have guns, so have we. You have powder and lead, and so have we. Your men will fight, and so will ours—'til the last drop of Seminole blood has moistened the dust of his hunting ground."

This was the message of defiance sent by Osceola in 1834 to General D. L. Clinch, the commander of the Army in Florida. It was he who led the Seminoles in their second war with the United States in which they were nearly exterminated. Had it not been for the Everglades, where they could hide out, there would not be a single Seminole in Florida today.

Osceola was the most famous of all Seminoles and one of the greatest and most famous of all American Indians. He was a Creek, born in Georgia, who came to live among the Seminoles when he was four years old. He grew up as any Seminole boy, and he was a skilled hunter and lover of sports.

Osceola was not a chief, and he was never elected to chieftaincy. He was a great warrior and an outstanding leader. He was and is the hero of all the Seminole people. He first came to attention during the council held with the tribe in an effort to induce them to sign the treaty consenting to their removal to the West. Some of the Seminoles had already gone, but these were the holdouts who refused to leave.

Osceola stepped to the council table. With flashing eyes, he drew his knife and stabbed it through the treaty papers. He cried out in a loud voice: "This land is ours. This is the way we will sign all such treaties."

It was not long before the war broke out. Osceola hid his fighting men in the swamps, from which he attacked and harassed the soldiers wherever he could find them. He was both feared and respected, and the troops were unable to win any victories against him.

Two years later, after desperate fighting, Osceola was captured while meeting with Army officers under a flag of truce. He and other Seminole leaders were put in prison, but the war continued for another six years.

Shortly before the death of Osceola, George Catlin, the famous artist, painted his portrait. The picture shows him to be a fine-looking young man, fairly tall and slender. He wore three ostrich plumes in his turban, and his clothing was of colored calico. Around his waist he wore a handsome handwoven sash. Another, with small silver ornaments, crisscrossed his chest, where three silver crescents were hung. On his legs were deerskin leggings tied around with woven garters. Osceola's hair was bobbed and banged on the forehead.

49

When he knew that he was dying, Osceola sent for the Seminole chiefs, for the officers of the fort where he was held prisoner, and for his two wives and his children. He put on the clothes that are shown in the portrait and laid his knife by his side. He painted one half of his face, neck, the backs of his hands, and the handle of his knife bright red. This was done when the oath of war was taken by the Seminoles. In spirit, Osceola was still at war with the white man.

When fully dressed, he lay down on his bed and placed his knife on his breast. In a moment, he was gone.

Osceola was buried with full military honors, and even those who had been his enemies spoke of him in highest terms as a man of gallantry and one who deserved a better fate. He never harmed women or children, but said to his warriors: "Spare the women and children. It is not upon them that we make war or draw the scalping knife. It is upon men. Let us act like men."

There are more places named for Osceola in this country than for any other Indian. Twenty towns, three counties, two townships, one borough, two lakes, two mountains, one state park, and one national forest, scattered over twenty-two states, are named Osceola.

Of those who fought with Osceola, the best known were Coacoochee, or Wild Cat, Micanopy, Billy Bowlegs, Alligator, and Jumper.

Wild Cat escaped from prison by climbing eighteen feet to the top of his cell, where there was a small opening. He crawled through and dropped into the moat below. Although he was hurt, he was able to get away.

Seventeen others escaped with him. They had starved themselves for weeks so that they could squeeze through the opening in the wall. They finally made their way back to their people.

11
The Fighting Ends

When Wild Cat escaped from prison, he once more took up the fight and led the Seminoles until they were so few they could no longer resist the soldiers. The fiercest battle of all took place on Christmas Day, 1837. In hand-to-hand fighting, 480 Seminoles under Alligator, Wild Cat, and Billy Bowlegs, fought an army of 1,100 men under General Zachary Taylor. The battle lasted three hours, and 28 soldiers were killed and more than 100 wounded. The Seminoles lost only 14 men before they disappeared into their swamps.

As the war neared its close, there were 8,000 soldiers in the field. One by one, the Indian leaders were captured or surrendered and were sent to Indian Territory with their followers. Billy Bowlegs and Aripeka, a medicine man, stayed in the Everglades with those who said they would never leave and who remained undefeated. Finally, Bowlegs and 165 of his people agreed to go, but Aripeka stayed on.

Some of the Seminoles went to Mexico rather than settle on the land selected by the United States in Indian Territory. Wild Cat was one of these, and he died in Mexico.

The Creek Indians set aside some of their lands in Oklahoma for the Seminoles who were to govern them-

selves. Micanopy was chosen the chief and leader. But the Civil War was to bring further hardship, and the pressures brought by North and South divided the Indians.

John Jumper, the son of the old chief, was the leader of the group who sided with the Confederates. He became a colonel in the Confederate Army. Under Bowlegs, those who were on the side of the North removed to Kansas, where they formed the Indian Home Guard Brigade to serve in the Union Army.

Even though they lost land and homes, the Seminoles fought with honor no matter which side they were on. Those who were in the Union forces were awarded $50,000, with which they bought more land from the Creeks.

With the Civil War over, the Seminoles settled down and established their capital at Wewoka. They elected John F. Brown as their chief, and a council of forty-two men. They had twelve tribal towns and two towns for their freed black slaves.

The Seminoles soon earned the reputation of being the most law-abiding of all Indian nations in Indian Territory. But they did not understand land or money values or landownership. They gradually lost their lands until little remained in Seminole hands.

12
The Seminoles Today

The Seminoles in Oklahoma are like any other citizen of that state. Their children go to public schools, and many of the Indian people are farmers, teachers, doctors, lawyers, ranchers, or civic leaders. The tribal council now has only thirty-six members. It still meets at Wewoka, and it advises the government on matters concerning Seminole welfare. There is little of Indian custom or tradition among these Indians.

There are more than 1,000 Seminoles living on four reservations in Florida which come under the United States government through the Bureau of Indian Affairs. A fifth reservation is owned by the State of Florida.

The Seminoles are divided into two groups, the Miccosukees and the Cow Creeks. The Miccosukees are the largest of the two, and most of them live in Everglades National Park. Of all Indian tribes, only they can say that they never signed a peace treaty and never were conquered. They are the descendants of those who were prepared to die rather than to leave Florida.

As they have always done, the Seminoles tend small gardens and raise cattle, pigs, and chickens. Many still live in the traditional chickee and still wear the colorful patchwork clothing. But life for the Seminoles is changing.

The Indians are still an independent people, and they prefer to keep to themselves; but the old barriers to friendship are gradually breaking down, and there is more acceptance of the white man's ways. If the Seminoles seem unfriendly, this is more shyness than actual hostility.

A few years ago six modern ranch homes were built for some of the leaders, and other Seminoles are now beginning to find these attractive. More are being built. Fast, shallow-draft airboats are replacing the ancient dugouts. Quite a few of the Indians have become members of the Baptist Church, although the Green Corn Dance is still held. This is not open to the public, and it takes place in a remote place where outsiders cannot find it.

There is still some opposition to education; but more and more Seminole children are now going to public school, and there are a few college graduates. There are government day schools on the reservations for small children and for those older ones who have not attended school before. Adult education classes are held for the grown-ups who have come into the schoolroom for the first time.

The Seminoles are citizens of the United States, as all Indians are. They can vote, hold public office, own land and personal property. They are citizens of Florida and obey the laws of that state, although they may hunt and fish on reservation land as they please. Most are full-blooded Indians.

A very healthy people, even when they live in the open chickees and in the humid swamp, most now use modern hospital facilities when necessary. They receive free health care through the Public Health Service. The people live long lives. It is not unusual to find individuals who have lived to be more than 100 years old in this tribe.

The Indians qualify for all welfare services. They have Social Security numbers, and some of the older people collect monthly pensions under this. Many of the Seminoles own cars, and the state provides them with specially designed licensed car tags.

The Seminoles have never received funds from the government, and they are somewhat indifferent to things that are "for free." Some prefer to purchase their license tags than to be given them.

There are no longer any chiefs in the tribe. The Miccosukees and Cow Creeks have organized under a constitution and have elected a governing council with a president.

In the past few years a million-dollar land development program, partly financed by the tribe, has developed more than 13,000 acres of improved pasture- and farm-lands. A timber management and sales program has been established. The tribe has set aside sixty-six acres of tribal land for an industrial park, and one manufacturing plant is now in operation.

Further plans call for the construction of a forty-unit motel, with restaurant, swimming pool, and golf course.

The Miccosukees have opened a fine restaurant near

Miami, financed in part through a government loan. They will also build a modern community center.

In 1968, for the first time in history the Seminoles elected a woman, Mrs. Betty Jumper, as chairman of the tribal council. She is the first Seminole to graduate from high school.

About thirty years ago the Seminoles became interested in cattle raising as a tribal industry. The government sold them a foundation herd of a few hundred head of beef cattle, and the government was completely paid off a year before payment was due. As the herd

58

increased, cattle was issued to heads of Seminole families as individual owners. For this, they signed promissory notes and took out livestock mortgages.

Stock raising is now a major industry in this one Indian community. The young men dress like cowboys and take great pride in their cowponies.

Some of the Indian men work with road gangs, in logging camps, or in seasonal labor. Both men and women are employed in state highway grass planting operations. Most of the palm leaves used in the churches of the country at Easter are picked by Seminole workers. The younger boys earn money by hunting frogs, which are bought by the large city restaurants which serve frogs' legs.

The making of Seminole crafts is a major source of income for the Seminoles. A craft center has been opened which attracts hundreds of tourists. The craftsmen make dolls dressed in Seminole style, wood carvings and small dugout canoes, beadwork, and basketry. The patchwork clothing has been adapted to modern styles and is produced in skirts, shirts and jackets, aprons and pinafores, head scarves and handbags.

Operated in connection with the craft center is a reproduction of an old-time Indian village illustrating Seminole life. There are other commercial tourist attraction villages where Seminoles are employed. One of the popular features is the alligator wrestling done by young men.

The Seminoles of Florida and Oklahoma have filed claims against the government for additional payment for the lands they once held. Their right to almost all the land in Florida has been allowed, and it is expected that the Indians will receive some $40,000,000 when matters are finally settled.

The Seminoles quietly follow their own way of life. They accept or refuse the advantages of modern civilization as they please. They will not allow any interference in their affairs, and they do not interfere with those who wish to follow new trails or to retain old habits.

It is readily seen, however, that younger Indians are becoming less different from the white children with whom they go to school and that there is a decided change in the attitudes of the older generation toward the white man.

Index

Alligator, 51, 53
Aripeka, 53
Autumn Hunting Dance, 44

Baptist Church, 56
Billy Bowlegs, 51, 53
Black drink, 45
Breath-Maker, 33, 36, 46
Brown, John F., 54
Bureau of Indian Affairs, 55

Catlin, George, 49
Chickees, 19
    life in, 21–24
Children, 29–32
Civil War, 54
Clinch, D. L., 48
Clothing, 25–28
Coacoochee, 51
Coontie, 22
Cow Creeks, 55, 57
Crafts, 60
Creek Indians, 53

Dugout canoes, 20

England, 12
Everglades, 16
    National Park, 55

Feather dance, 45
Florida, 8
    cession to United States, 12
    early Seminoles in, 11–12
    first Indians in, 8
Folk songs, 32
Folktales, 33–36
Food, 22–23

Green Corn Dance, 43, 44–47, 56

Indian Home Guard Brigade, 54
Indian Territory, 14, 53
Ishtohollo, 46

Jackson, Andrew, 12
Jumper, Betty, 58
Jumper, John, 51, 54

Land-development program, 57

Medicine man, 41–43
Micanopy, 51, 54
Miccosukees, 55, 57, 58

Osceola, 48-49, 51

Public Health Service, 57

Seminoles
    in chickees, 21–24
    and children, 29–32
    clothing of, 25–28
    and colonists, 12
    in Everglades, 16, 17 ff.
    on Florida reservation, 13–16
    and folktales, 33–36
    groups, 55
    health of, 57
    in Oklahoma, 54, 55
    origin of, 11
    village life of, 17–20
Sofkee, 22
Spain, 12
Spanish explorers, 8
Stickball, 37–40
Stock raising, 58–59
Storyteller, 32

Taylor, Zachary, 53
Tourist attraction villages, 60

Village life, 17–20

War, with United States, 48–51, 53
War medicine, 43
Wild Cat, 51, 53

Yo-He-Wah, 46–47

The Story of the SEMINOLE

is the latest volume in a series of authentic books about INDIAN NATIONS that have made significant contributions to our heritage and also are representative of particular cultures.

The Editors of *Country Beautiful* recommend the new titles, all written by Marion E. Gridley and published by G. P. Putnam's Sons in association with the Country Beautiful Corporation.

INDIAN NATIONS:
  The Story of the IROQUOIS
  The Story of the NAVAJO
  The Story of the SIOUX
  The Story of the HAIDA
  The Story of the SEMINOLE

The Author

MARION E. GRIDLEY has always been interested in Indian culture and is an adopted member of two tribes—the Omaha and the Winnebago. She and her parents founded the Indian Council Fire, a national Indian-interest organization of Indian and white membership, and Miss Gridley has served as executive secretary of the organization since its inception. Miss Gridley is the editor and publisher of *The Amerindian*, a bimonthly information bulletin on Indians. She is the author of beginning-to-read biographies of *Pontiac* and *Osceola* and has also written five books in the Putnam–Country Beautiful INDIAN NATIONS library—the *Sioux*, the *Navajo*, the *Haida*, the *Iroquois*, and the *Seminole*.

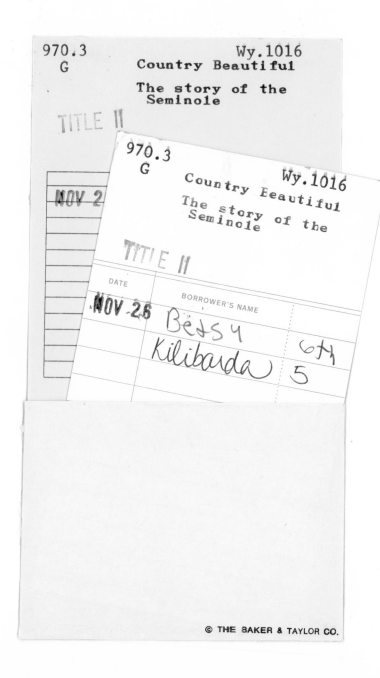

970.3   Wy.1016
G   Country Beautiful

            The story of the
            Seminole

TITLE II

970.3   Wy.1016
G   Country Beautiful
            The story of the
            Seminole

TITLE II

DATE	BORROWER'S NAME	
NOV 25	Betsy	6th
	Kilibarda	5

© THE BAKER & TAYLOR CO.